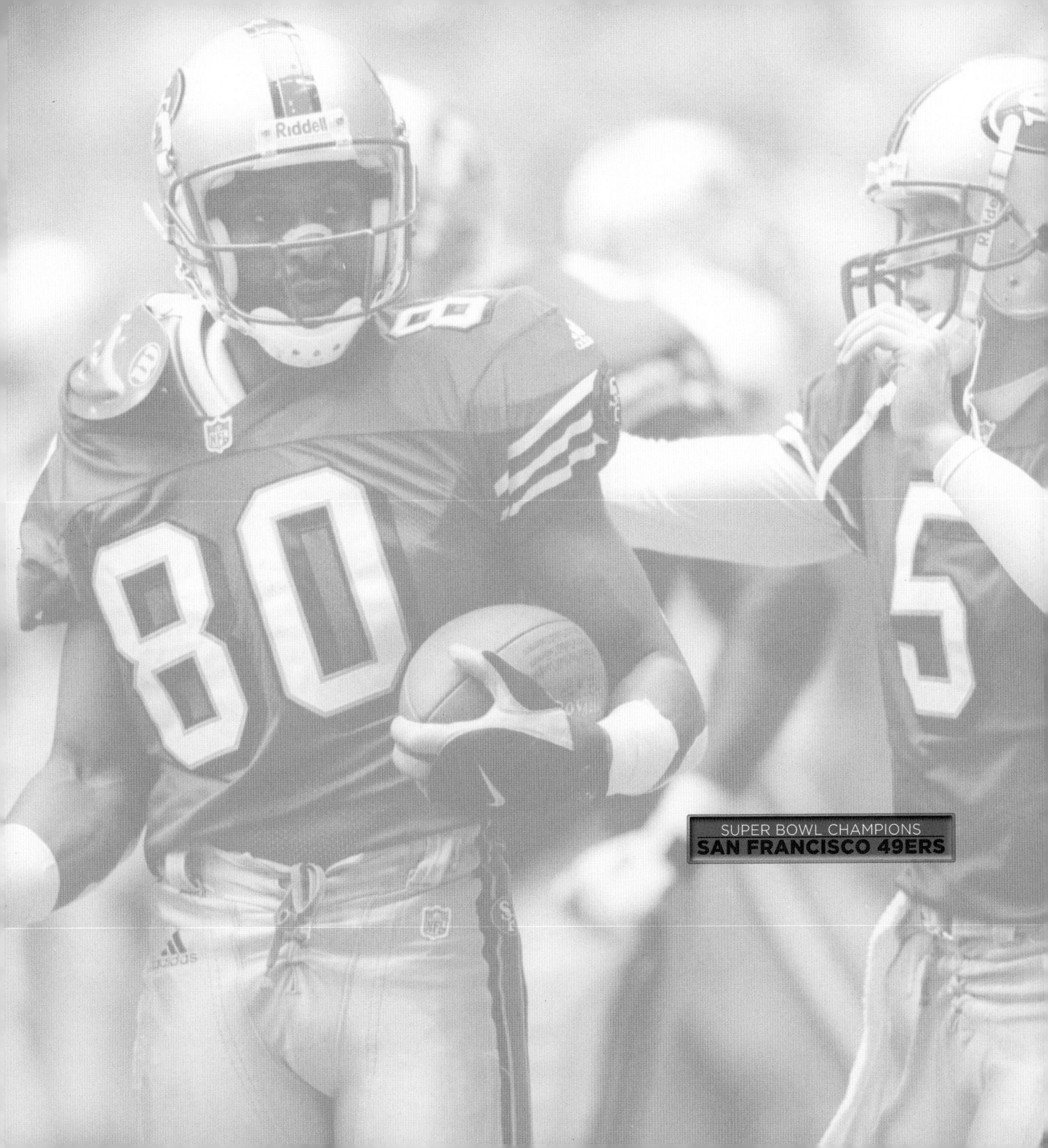
Riddell
80
SUPER BOWL CHAMPIONS
SAN FRANCISCO 49ERS

QUARTERBACK
COLIN KAEPERNICK

SUPER BOWL CHAMPIONS

SAN FRANCISCO 49ERS

AARON FRISCH

CREATIVE EDUCATION

Published by Creative Education
P.O. Box 227, Mankato, Minnesota 56002
Creative Education is an imprint of The Creative Company
www.thecreativecompany.us

Design and production by Blue Design
Art direction by Rita Marshall
Printed in the United States of America

Photographs by Getty Images (Mike Ehrmann, Otto Greule
Jr., Otto Greule Jr./Allsport, Leon Halip, Andy Hayt, Walter
Iooss Jr./Sports Illustrated, Heinz Kluetmeier/Sports
Illustrated, Kirby Lee/NFL, Peter Read Miller/Sports
Illustrated, MPS/NFL, Frank Rippon/NFL, George Rose,
Travel Ink, Greg Trott, Michael Zagaris)

Library of Congress Cataloging-in-Publication Data
Frisch, Aaron.
San Francisco 49ers / Aaron Frisch.
p. cm. — (Super bowl champions)
Includes index.
Summary: An elementary look at the San Francisco 49ers
professional football team, including its formation in 1946,
most memorable players, Super Bowl championships, and
stars of today.
ISBN 978-1-60818-387-6
1. San Francisco 49ers (Football team)—History—Juvenile
literature. I. Title.

GV956.S3F75 2014
796.332'640979461—dc23   2013014838

First Edition
9 8 7 6 5 4 3 2 1

RUNNING BACK
FRANK GORE

RONNIE LOTT / 1981-90

Ronnie was a fierce safety. He was famous for his hard hits and caused a lot of fumbles.

TABLE OF CONTENTS

SOUND IT OUT

McELHENNY: *MAK-ul-heh-nee*

DEFENSIVE TACKLE
LEO NOMELLINI

A GOLDEN TEAM

In 1849, many people went to California to look for gold. These people were called "49ers." California still has 49ers today—the San Francisco 49ers football team!

HUGH McELHENNY / 1952-60

Hugh was a fast running back in the 1950s. His 49ers teammates nicknamed him "The King."

WELCOME TO SAN FRANCISCO

San Francisco is a city in California. San Francisco has many big hills. It is next to the ocean and has a famous bridge called the Golden Gate Bridge.

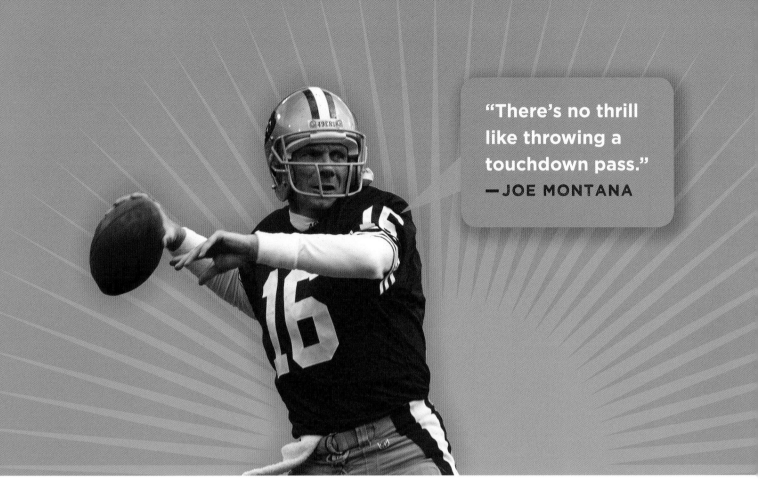

"There's no thrill like throwing a touchdown pass."
—JOE MONTANA

THE TEAM OF THE '80s

The 49ers were the best team in the National Football League (NFL) in the 1980s. They won four Super Bowls! People called San Francisco the "Team of the '80s."

DWIGHT CLARK

1979–87

Dwight was a sure-handed tight end. He made a famous catch in the 1981 playoffs.

QUARTERBACK
JOHN BRODIE

THE 49ERS' STORY

The 49ers started out in 1946. Players like quarterback John Brodie were fun to watch. But the 49ers did not get to the playoffs very often in the 1950s and 1960s.

In 1978, the 49ers hired coach Bill Walsh. The next year, they added quarterback Joe Montana. After the 1981 season, the 49ers won their first Super Bowl!

BILL WALSH AND
JOE MONTANA

JERRY RICE

he 49ers kept on winning. They won three more Super Bowls after the 1984, 1988, and 1989 seasons. Stars like wide receiver Jerry Rice scored many touchdowns.

ROGER CRAIG / 1983-90

Roger joined the 49ers in 1983. He was a tough running back who was very hard to bring down.

"Football is a unique sport. There is no statistic, no touchdown, or passing yard that is accomplished by a single person."
—STEVE YOUNG

JIM HARBAUGH

uarterback Steve Young replaced Joe Montana. Steve led the 49ers to another championship. He threw six touchdown passes to help win Super Bowl XXIX (29).

By 2010, the 49ers were a bad team. But then new coach Jim Harbaugh helped make San Francisco a **contender** again.

VERNON DAVIS

2006–present

Vernon was a fast tight end. He was known as one of the strongest tight ends in the NFL, too.

n 2013, San Francisco fans had fun watching fast wide receiver Michael Crabtree and quarterback Colin Kaepernick. They hoped their team would soon strike gold and win a sixth Super Bowl!

MICHAEL CRABTREE

FACTS FILE

CONFERENCE/DIVISION:
National Football
Conference, West Division

TEAM COLORS:
Burgundy and gold

HOME STADIUM:
Candlestick Park

SUPER BOWL VICTORIES:
XVI, January 24, 1982
  26–21 over Cincinnati
  Bengals
XIX, January 20, 1985
  38–16 over Miami Dolphins
XXIII, January 22, 1989
  20–16 over Cincinnati
  Bengals
XXIV, January 28, 1990
  55–10 over Denver
  Broncos
XXIX, January 29, 1995
  49–26 over San Diego
  Chargers

NFL WEBSITE FOR KIDS:
http://nflrush.com

PATRICK WILLIS / 2007–present

Patrick was a hard-hitting linebacker. He made 137 tackles when he was just a **rookie**.

GLOSSARY

contender — a talented team that has a good chance of winning a championship

playoffs — games that the best teams play after a season to see who the champion will be

rookie — a player in his first season

sure-handed — good at catching or holding onto the football

INDEX